Investigating
TERRORIST
ATTACKS AT THE
HANDS OF ISIS

BRIDEY HEING

Rosen
YA™

New York

Published in 2018 by The Rosen Publishing Group, Inc.
29 East 21st Street, New York, NY 10010

Library of Congress Cataloging-in-Publication Data

Names: Heing, Bridey, author.
Title: Investigating terrorist attacks at the hands of ISIS / Bridey Heing.
Description: New York, NY : The Rosen Publishing Group, Inc., 2018. | Series: Terrorism in the 21st century : causes and effects | Includes bibliographical references and index.
Identifiers: LCCN 2016059971 | ISBN 9781508174646 (library bound book)
Subjects: LCSH: IS (Organization) | Terrorism—Religious aspects—Islam.
Classification: LCC HV6433.I722 H45 2018 | DDC 363.325/165—dc23
LC record available at https://lccn.loc.gov/2016059971

Manufactured in China

On the cover: An Islamic State of Iraq and Syria (ISIS) flag is displayed in the background as a soldier guards a town recently recaptured from the terrorist organization. ISIS has become a major terrorist threat in recent years, not only in Iraq and Syria but also across the world.

Contents

Introduction

The Islamic State of Iraq and Syria, or ISIS, has emerged as one of the most critical terrorist organizations of the twenty-first century. Since its foundation in 2013, the group has carried out attacks across the Middle East, and more recently claimed responsibility for attacks in Europe and the United States. The group has hundreds of foreign followers and leaders of the organization have called for supporters to carry out attacks in their own countries, making them a concern to governments around the world.

ISIS started as an offshoot of al-Qaeda called al-Qaeda in Iraq (or AQI) in 2004. Although originally established to fight against the United States in Iraq, the group became active in Syria when fighting began between Bashar al-Assad's government and protesters in 2011. Tension with al-Qaeda's leadership

ISIS, or the Islamic State, has established itself as a formidable force in Syria and Iraq, relying on terrorism to control populations.

eventually led the group to break away and establish themselves independently, absorbing other extremist groups in Iraq and Syria. In 2013, leader Abu Bakr al-Baghdadi announced the formation of the Islamic State in Iraq and Syria and by the end of that year had taken the Iraqi city of Fallujah.

Since then, ISIS has taken control of portions of Iraq and Syria, establishing their "capital" in Raqqa in northern Syria. Under Baghdadi, a secretive leader who has not been seen in video or photographs since 2014, the group has styled itself as a caliphate, or an Islamic theocratic state. But the group is notoriously brutal, using terror and fear to govern the areas they hold and targeting civilians in wide-ranging attacks. Since the group's earliest days, they have recruited from countries around the world by using social media and propaganda, and today they have supporters across the globe.

The United States and allied nations have worked to retake ISIS-held territory, pushing the organization out of former strongholds. But their international following has made it possible for the group to carry out attacks in the West, including in Belgium and France. Supporters have also carried out attacks in the group's name in the United States, Germany, and the United Kingdom, although it is not believed that ISIS played a role in planning these attacks. ISIS and its affiliate groups have also targeted civilians across Africa, where it is fighting al-Qaeda for dominance, as well as Asia.

Through these attacks, ISIS has sought to create an image of power and to establish themselves as the leader of jihadist extremists around the world. These jihadist extremists follow an extreme interpretation of Islam in order to wage war on those who do not share their beliefs. The group's ability to recruit online and their willingness to embrace attacks carried out in their name have made them a threat to populations around the world, but experts also believe this could be a sign that the group is struggling to hold onto power in their former strongholds. Experts argue that air strikes and attacks against them in Syria and Iraq have forced the group to rethink their strategy, shifting away from taking territory to targeting civilians overseas.

This book will discuss the history of ISIS, how they coordinate or influence terrorist attacks around the world, and what is being done to counter their ability to carry out these attacks. We will also explore the future of ISIS and what experts say could defeat them.

CHAPTER ONE

The History of ISIS

The rise of ISIS was fast and unprecedented, with the group growing into one of the world's most powerful terrorist organizations in the space of just a few years. Since it was established less than twenty years ago, the group has been known by several names, held and lost key cities in the Middle East and Africa, and has built a network of supporters around the world.

In Syria, ISIS has taken advantage of chaos due to an ongoing civil war to capture territory and weapons, like this jet.

ISIS is a Salafist jihadist group rooted in a violent interpretation of Sunni Islam. In this sense they are similar to groups like Boko Haram in Africa or al-Qaeda in the Middle East, which share similar ideologies. What has set ISIS apart, however, is their reliance on extreme violence and their military capabilities. The group does not recognize modern readings or innovations in Islam, and wants to return to a way of faith that reflects the early days of the Islamic Empire. ISIS is also a millenarian group, meaning that they believe an apocalyptic event is coming in the near future. Their propaganda references the apocalypse often, and the group seems to believe that their existence fulfills a prophecy that signals the final Day of Judgment. The group is able to use this message of prophecy to draw in recruits and justify their violence, as well as to motivate fighters to carry out suicide missions.

ISLAMIC SECTS

There are two major sects, or branches, of Islam that Muslims follow: Sunni and Shia Islam. Sunni Muslims make up 85 percent of the global population of Muslims, while Shiites make up approximately 15 percent of all Muslims. While extremism can exist in any branch of any religion, most of the major Islamic terrorist organizations, including al-Qaeda and ISIS, are based on fundamentalist interpretations of Sunni Islam. Likewise, the Salafi movement is an ultra-conservative movement that developed within Sunni Islam. Salafists reject modernism and Western influence, and desire a return to Islam's roots in the seventh century when the Prophet Muhammad (the founder of Islam) first received the word of God. These fundamentalist interpretations are not representative of Islam or of the majority of Muslims' beliefs today.

Al-Qaeda in Iraq

In the early 2000s, al-Qaeda was the most powerful terrorist organization in the Middle East. They carried out the September 11 attacks against the United States in 2001 and engaged US forces frequently in combat in Afghanistan. When the United States invaded Iraq in 2003 to topple the Saddam Hussein government, al-Qaeda sought a foothold in the country to fight US forces. Jordanian fighter Abu Musab al-Zarqawi established al-Qaeda in Iraq in 2004 by pledging his Iraq-based group, Jama'at al-Tawhid w'al-Jihad, to al-Qaeda.

Zarqawi tried to find support among Sunni Iraqis, who felt largely disenfranchised by the government. This was because Sunni Muslims, a minority group that had been in power under Hussein's regime, were forced out of government positions in favor of the Shiite majority. The United States had supported the creation of "awakening councils," which sought to reconcile the largely Shiite government of Prime Minister Nouri al-Maliki with Sunni populations. These councils were successful enough that al-Qaeda in Iraq was unable to gain significant backing under Zarqawi. The group carried out attacks against Shia holy sites in an attempt to create conflict between Iraq's Sunnis and Shiites, but was unable to sow the kind of unrest that would allow the group to grow. Zarqawi was killed in US air strikes in 2006, making way for new leadership under Abu Ayyub al-Masri and Abu Omar al-Baghdadi. Baghdadi gave a new name to al-Qaeda in Iraq: the Islamic State in Iraq (ISI).

Islamic State in Iraq

As the Islamic State in Iraq the group became more brutal, which caused tension with al-Qaeda. Al-Qaeda was opposed to indiscriminate attacks

Abu Bakr al-Baghdadi is the leader of ISIS, but he is rarely seen in public or on video and little is known about him.

against Muslims, but the Islamic State in Iraq refused to alter their tactics. Both Abu Ayyub al-Masri and Abu Omar al-Baghdadi were killed in air strikes in 2010, and Abu Bakr al-Baghdadi (who was unrelated to Abu Omar al-Baghdadi) took control of ISI.

Under the second Baghdadi ISI became stronger, and started carrying out multiple attacks each month in Iraq. After the outbreak of civil war in Syria in 2011, Baghdadi set up al-Nusra Front, another wing of al-Qaeda fighting against Syrian government forces. The group quickly became one of the most powerful in the conflict, but their loyalties were split between al-Qaeda leadership and Baghdadi. This created tension when Baghdadi attempted to gain control of al-Nusra Front in 2013. Although leaders of these terrorist groups rejected his claim of merging ISI and al-Nusra Front, some fighters did leave al-Nusra Front to fight on behalf of Baghdadi's Islamic State in Iraq and Syria.

Islamic State in Iraq and Syria

The creation of ISIS was announced by Baghdadi in August 2013. By December of that year the group was extremely active in Iraq. Baghdadi was able to exploit the tension between the Shia government and the Sunni population,

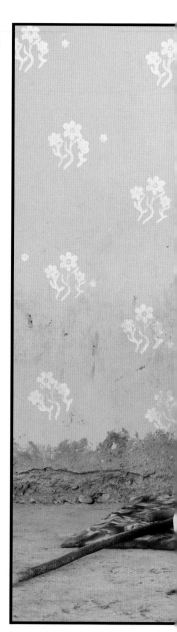

particularly among those who were loyal to Saddam Hussein and who opposed the US-led operation to remove Hussein from power.
ISIS grew quickly and with their newly increased ranks took control of the city of Fallujah.

Yazidis, an ethnic and religious minority, have been the target of ISIS violence, including starvation and sexual violence.

In June 2014, the group took the northern city of Mosul, located near the capital city of Baghdad. Taking Mosul put ISIS on the map as a terrorist organization capable of challenging those in power, with goals that stretched beyond carrying out attacks on behalf of causes. Their steady march south toward Baghdad, during which they targeted civilians and raided banks and military bases for currency and weapons, underlined the group's ambition and capabilities.

Meanwhile, the group was also active in Syria and northern Iraq, claiming territory and engaging government forces in combat. In August 2014, ISIS began targeting the Yazidi minority in northern Iraq and parts of Syria, carrying out what has been called a genocide against the population. Yazidis are an ethnic and religious Kurdish minority and ISIS considers their faith illegitimate. As a result, ISIS has captured and massacred thousands of Yazidis, making many of them slaves, sexually assaulting women, and forcing thousands to convert to their interpretation of Sunni Islam. The Yazidis are not the only population ISIS has targeted—the group has also massacred Shiites and Christians in territory they hold—but the Yazidis's history of persecution and the violence used against them are some of the first at this level known to the international community.

It was clear by mid 2014 that ISIS was a group that the international community as a whole needed to counter, but how to do so was unclear. As the international community began grappling with that question, ISIS declared itself the Islamic State.

The Islamic State

The Islamic State is designed to be a caliphate, or an empire governed by Islamic law. Although the group itself uses this term, the international community does not as a way to reject the group's interpretation of Islam.

AL-BAGHDADI: THE LEADER OF ISIS

Abu Bakr al-Baghdadi became the leader of ISIS in 2010, and under him the group has become one of the most powerful terrorist organizations in the world. But little is known about the man himself, who appears infrequently in public or on video. He was born Awwad Ibrahim Ali al-Badri al-Samarrai in Iraq in 1971, and according to some accounts he holds a doctorate from the Islamic University in Baghdad. Intelligence analysts believe he was an Islamic preacher around 2003, when the United States invaded Iraq, and soon after the invasion became involved in militant Islam. He was captured by US forces in 2005, and for four years was held in a prison camp in southern Iraq. It is believed that he met al-Qaeda fighters in this camp, and those relationships led to his involvement with the group that would become ISIS. Since taking control of the group he has maintained a low public profile, but his reputation for strategy and brutality has made him the premiere leader of the global terrorist network. When he declared the formation of the Islamic State caliphate, he declared himself leader of all Muslims, a claim rejected by Muslim leaders and worshipers around the world.

Instead, the group is called ISIS, ISIL, or Daesh. Some media outlets also call the group the "so-called Islamic State."

Since 2014, the group has taken territory in Syria and lost territory in Iraq, meaning that their borders are constantly shifting. ISIS has been able to use the chaos of Syria to their advantage, extending their influence beyond the territory they control even as Iraqi forces reclaim towns and cities that were once held by the group. The group has also become more active in Africa and has worked to recruit fighters and supporters overseas.

Those who have been saved from ISIS-held territory have told of extreme violence, strict gender-based restrictions, and an atmosphere of terror. Mass executions are common in ISIS-held territory, as is sexual slavery. The group has also used civilians as human shields to deter US and ally air strikes.

In early 2015, the US Director of National Intelligence estimated that there were between 20,000 and 32,000 ISIS fighters in ISIS held territory, but it is unclear how many of those have died in fighting or air strikes, or how many were forced to join the group. It is also believed that the majority of fighters are not from Iraq or Syria, with an estimated 28,000 fighters joining from around the world as of October 2015. Of that number, about 5,000 are believed to be from western countries and around 250 are believed to be US citizens.

CHAPTER TWO

Attacks by ISIS in the Islamic World

The ideology, or political and religious beliefs, that drives ISIS is in part built on a belief that the group can conquer the Islamic world and that all Muslims are required by sharia law to be loyal followers

ISIS has targeted numerous Middle Eastern countries in attempts to undermine the state, including carrying out dozens of attacks in Iraq.

of Baghdadi. This has led the group to carry out numerous attacks around the world, but most prominently in Muslim-majority countries, especially in the Middle East and Africa. ISIS has carried out many attacks in recent years, but the means and motivations for each attack vary. Some are carried out to claim territory, while others are designed to position ISIS as the strongest terrorist organization in an area. Attacks are also carried out to undermine leadership in regional states, such as Egypt.

ISIS Affiliates

To understand how ISIS carries out attacks around the Islamic world, it is important to understand how ISIS's network of affiliates works. Affiliated groups are organizations that have pledged allegiance to ISIS, but might still work independently. Many groups that affiliate with ISIS change their names to reflect their location in the ISIS network. For example, in Yemen, the ISIS-affiliated militant group is called Sanaa Province, while in Libya groups are called Tripoli Province, Barqa Province, and Fezzan Province. Boko Haram, a powerful militant group based in Nigeria, still goes by the name under which it became famous, but is formally called the Islamic State West Africa Province.

Affiliates are a tool many terrorist organizations use to carry out attacks and spread their influence around the world. Most terrorist organizations have a small core group of leaders and many do not have large numbers of fighters. Affiliates allow that small number to project their influence much wider than they could by themselves, while also allowing for resource and training sharing. Through affiliates, groups are able to show their strength and gain control of areas outside of their immediate vicinity, which can help them survive military campaigns in their primary territory. For example, the ISIS affiliate in Libya was believed to be a secondary base of operations when ISIS's core territories in Iraq and Syria began decreasing. Analysts believed that if Raqqa, ISIS's de facto capital, falls, then the group could relocate leadership to the coast of Libya.

ISIS Territory

Terrorism, or the use of violence and fear to achieve political goals, is not isolated to one-off attacks by ISIS. In fact, the group uses these acts to maintain control of populations in territories they hold. ISIS leadership sees itself as a state and wants to govern according to their strict interpretation of sharia law. In order to do so, the group has used violence against civilians and those accused of crimes to maintain control through fear.

Examples of terrorist activity within ISIS territory include the persecution of the Yazidis, many of whom are given the choice to either die or convert to ISIS's ideology, and the way they punish criminals or those seen as disloyal to the group. According to witnesses who have fled ISIS controlled areas, the group uses violent and public punishments, such as stonings, beatings, or executions, to keep their populations from violating their laws. These stories are supported by videos the group has released showing brutal executions, a tactic designed to make others fear them.

The Middle East, North Africa & Asia

ISIS has carried out numerous attacks throughout the Middle East, North Africa, and Asia since 2013, both to claim territory and to undermine leadership. The group has affiliates that have carried out attacks in Yemen, Saudi Arabia, Afghanistan, Libya, and Egypt, and the group is believed to have been involved in attacks in Tunisia, Syria, Iraq, Kuwait, Lebanon, Bangladesh, Indonesia, Kazakhstan, Malaysia, and Pakistan.

The attacks the group has carried out in Iraq have been aimed at both taking new territory, as can be seen in their attacks in 2013, and targeting civilians in non-ISIS held areas in order to further their ideological aims. In Iraq, the group often used multiple attacks across multiple cities to create a sense of chaos and a show of power, many of which have killed hundreds and injured hundreds more in only one day. Since 2013, however, Iraq has not been the primary focus of highly organized attacks and the group has instead focused on suicide or car bombings

IN MEMORIAM
This plaque is dedicated to all the guests who lost their lives in the terrorist attack at the Imperial Marhaba Hotel on June 26th, 2015.

This memorial in Tunisia commemorates an attack at a resort that targeted Western tourists.

in the country. In July 2016, the group carried out a series of bombings near Baghdad that killed 325 people and wounded over 225, the group's deadliest attack since a May 2013 attack that killed over 400 and wounded over 700 in cities across Iraq.

ISIS V. AL-QAEDA: A DEADLY STRUGGLE

Until ISIS emerged as the powerful organization it has become, al-Qaeda was the dominant jihadist group in the world with affiliates across the Middle East, Asia, and Africa. Although both groups are Sunni and Salafist, they differ significantly in goals and tactics. ISIS seeks to conquer and govern through brutal violence, while al-Qaeda seeks to push the United States out of the Middle East but not to govern themselves. ISIS got its earliest start as a branch of al-Qaeda in Iraq, but disagreement with al-Qaeda leadership eventually pushed ISIS to become an independent entity in 2013. Since then, the group has challenged al-Qaeda's strength in multiple arenas, including the Syrian Civil War, the Yemeni Civil War, and in West Africa. In Africa, the fight between the two organizations has been deadly, as both have attempted to show their strength by carrying out attacks. But competing with ISIS has proved difficult for al-Qaeda, a group led by older militants and seen as largely out of touch with technology and the power of social media to recruit supporters. The same infighting that led to the creation of ISIS continues to be an issue for both groups.

Egypt has been another key target of ISIS attacks in the Middle East. The group's affiliate in the Sinai Peninsula, called Sinai Province, has claimed responsibility for multiple high profile attacks, including the 2015 downing of Metrojet Flight 9268 en route to Russia. In Libya, Pakistan, Saudi Arabia, and elsewhere, the group has targeted security forces and military bases, while in Afghanistan, Lebanon, Bangladesh, and other countries, the group has targeted civilians. In some cases, such as the 2015 attack on the Port El Kantaoui resort in Tunisia and the 2016 attack on the Bella Vista hotel in Egypt, the group has targeted foreign tourists.

Expansion into Africa

In 2016, ISIS began expanding their influence in Africa through alliances with key terrorist organizations across the continent. A group called the Islamic State in East Africa has been active in Mali, while Jahba East Africa is a newly emerged group that is believed to be made up of former al-Shabaab fighters now loyal to Baghdadi. In western Africa, Boko Haram has aligned with ISIS despite having previously been aligned with al-Qaeda. The level of involvement ISIS has with these groups isn't known, but it is believed that a foothold in Africa could help the group remain active even if allied forces retake their territory in the Middle East.

The rise of ISIS in Africa has been checked by a few factors, including the already well-established presence of al-Qaeda. With multiple terrorist organizations vying for influence and power, it is more difficult for ISIS to rise to prominence the way they have in the Middle East. Instead, ISIS and its affiliates have to fight other terrorist organizations. This is particularly true in places like Mali and

ISIS has become more active in Africa in recent years, where alliances have pitted them against al-Qaeda in a fight for influence.

Burkina Faso, where several terrorist groups are already located and seeking dominance.

Africa has also been the focus of international efforts to stem terrorist organizations, including Boko Haram, al-Shabaab, and the Lord's Resistance Army. Although these campaigns have been unable to fully stop terrorist organizations from emerging or carrying out attacks, the infrastructure exists to combat them. Terrorist organizations like ISIS thrive in chaos, just as ISIS did in Syria, and Africa's established anti-terrorist campaigns have made if difficult for ISIS affiliates on the continent to make sustained chaos.

CHAPTER THREE

Attacks by ISIS in the West

For most of its short history, ISIS has been focused on conquering territory in the Middle East and North Africa, taking focus away from the West. This is part of the group's ultimate goal of establishing an Islamic state that controls Muslim-majority areas and then conquering non-Muslim majority countries. But analysts suspect that tactic changed when ISIS began losing territory to international forces. In late 2015, the group began carrying out or coordinating larger attacks in countries it previously hadn't targeted, including France, Turkey, and Lebanon. Before this, in May 2014, the group had also started encouraging supporters to carry out attacks in their own countries, and some United States citizens are believed to have been inspired by the group even if they were not directly in contact with ISIS.

ISIS in the West

ISIS does not have a formal presence in the West, but it does frequently threaten Western states in video messages and other communications. Conquering the West is one of the group's stated goals, although experts

Belgium was attacked in 2016 by ISIS loyalists. The small country has a relatively high number of citizens who have joined the group.

do not believe ISIS is capable of doing so. For now, anti-Western rhetoric is one way for the group to impress possible supporters, many of whom blame Western intervention in the Middle East for the cycle of conflict and suffering that has taken hold in many countries. Even if ISIS isn't in the West, Western countries are a significant part of their strategy.

Since 2015, that strategy has expanded to include large-scale attacks on Western targets. Although ISIS does not have a formal affiliate in any Western countries as it does in parts of the Middle East and Africa, the group has been able to draw supporters from countries like Australia, the United States, and the United Kingdom. ISIS has also been able to inspire attacks across the world, and has masterminded high profile and high casualty attacks in Belgium and France.

ISIS is able to connect with possible supporters in a number of ways, including through social media. The group has proven skilled at using the internet to spread propaganda and contact possible recruits, creating new accounts even as known accounts are suspended. Radicalization, or the process by which an individual comes to accept extreme and often violent beliefs, can take multiple years, and ISIS is willing to put in that time to lure fighters to join their ranks. Although the process of radicalization is still little understood, it has made ISIS a critical challenge for states in the West, who are working to stem the flow of fighters across borders and discourage possible ISIS supporters from carrying out attacks on their own soil.

Attacks in the West

ISIS supporters began carrying out attacks in the West in 2014, with an attack on the Jewish Museum of Belgium in Brussels that May. The gunman, who opened fire at the museum and killed four, was later found

ISIS AND SOCIAL MEDIA

Of the many weapons ISIS has, social media has proven to be one of the hardest to counter and the most important. Through sites like Twitter, Facebook, and Instagram, the group is able to contact possible recruits from around the world and spread their propaganda. In 2015, over 10,000 ISIS accounts were shut down on Twitter alone, and most of those were able to simply by create a new account. According to the Independent Journal Review, there are an estimated 46,000 ISIS Twitter accounts active at any given time. Through Twitter and other sites, the group is able to make contact with potential recruits and then privately message with them over time, slowly encouraging the potential recruit to radicalize. On social media the group shares public works and military successes, both of which are intended to highlight the group's strength and continued growth. This strategy is working: as of early 2016, an estimated 30,000 people have been radicalized online and then traveled to the Middle East to join the ranks of ISIS.

with a paper bearing the name of the Islamic State. This kind of vague association was common in early attacks, which were often carried out by lone attackers targeting a small number of people. The Brussels attack was the most deadly ISIS-linked attack in the West in 2014, and other attacks in Australia, the United States, and France resulted in no fatalities. At that time, ISIS was more focused on expanding their territory in the Middle East than they were on coordinating attacks on the West.

The Bataclan was the scene of a deadly hostage situation during an hours-long attack in Paris carried out by ISIS loyalists.

But that changed in 2015, when ISIS was under fire from allied forces and air strikes. An attack in Denmark in February killed two and injured five, and a series of bombings across Europe killed 139 and injured over 600. In November of that year, a group of ISIS attackers carried out a widespread attack in Paris, killing 130 people and injuring 386. The eleven attackers, led by Belgian national Abdelhamid Abaaoud, were all European nationals or citizens who had been radicalized by ISIS. The attack included suicide bombings and shootings at restaurants and a stadium, and the taking of the Bataclan nightclub, where attackers opened fire on the crowd and took hostages. Nine of those involved died during the attack or in firefights with the police. The two others, Salah Abdeslam and Mohamed Abrini, were arrested the next year.

Abdelhamid Abaaoud was among those who died during the attack, but he was believed to also have had a hand in planning a March 2016 attack on a metro station and airport in Brussels, Belgium. Like the attack in Paris the year before, the Brussels attack included multiple simultaneous suicide bombings, this time targeting the Maalbeek metro station and the Brussels Airport. Three attackers carried out the bombings, killing 32 people and injuring 340. Although little is known about how Abaaoud became linked to ISIS, it is believed he may have spent time in Syria. He was also linked to failed plots in France, and authorities believe he joined ISIS in 2013 and took the alias Abu Umar al-Baljiki. This direct link to ISIS isn't present in all attacks the group has claimed or all the attacks in which the attacker pledges allegiance to ISIS. Another attack in July of 2016 was carried out in Nice, France, when Mohamed Lahouaiej Bouhlel drove a truck through Bastille Day celebrations, killing 84 people and injuring hundreds, but ISIS's claims of responsibility have not been verified and were roundly dismissed by French authorities.

Until the attack in Paris, it wasn't clear if ISIS was able to carry out the kinds of large-scale attacks in the West that counterterrorism experts suspected they may have wanted to and that had made al-Qaeda an international threat. These attacks were a show of strength that would help bolster morale among followers and target the West, creating concern among western leaders. It marked a turning point, signaling that ISIS was willing to plan and coordinate complex attacks from afar through foreign nationals who train with ISIS before being sent back to their home countries. Belgium and France, in particular, are considered areas of concern, with a large number of fighters believed to have left these countries to join ISIS.

ISIS Supporters in the United States

ISIS has not carried out the kind of attack on the United States that it did in Belgium or France. More common is the lone perpetrator attack, in which attackers cite allegiance to ISIS or ISIS claims responsibility for the attack afterward. The first attack of this kind took place in October 2014, when a man attempted to attack two police officers. He was killed by police before he could cause any fatalities. The following May another would-be attacker targeted the Curtis Culwell Center in Garland, Texas, where he wounded one person before being killed by security forces.

In 2015, a San Bernardino couple, Rizwan Farook and Tashfeen Malik, shot dozens of people after pledging support to ISIS. The attack killed fourteen people and wounded twenty-four, although authorities are unsure if there is any direct link between the couple and ISIS. Similarly, in 2016, Omar Mateen called authorities during his shooting at the Pulse nightclub in Orlando, Florida, to declare his support for ISIS. With fifty fatalities, it was the largest terrorist attack on US soil since the September 11 attacks in 2001.

Declaring support for ISIS is not the same thing as being directly guided by ISIS, although that can get lost in the shock following an attack. In the case of Mateen, Farook, and Malik, and other attackers who declared support for ISIS, it is not believed that they were acting on specific orders from ISIS. Rather these individuals responded to the group's calls for attacks in different countries. By claiming the attacks, as ISIS often does, the group is able to use the violence as a show of power without having to be involved with the planning. This is one of the reasons ISIS is so difficult to combat; even though they do not have a significant foothold in the United States, supporters willing to carry out isolated attacks on their behalf can create the illusion that the group is more coordinated than it actually is.

As of late 2015, there were around 900 active investigations into possible ISIS supporters in the United States, and as of late 2016, 106 cases had been brought against United States citizens due to

In San Bernardino, a memorial is held for victims of the terrorist attack, which was carried out without clear guidance from ISIS.

their connections with ISIS. One of those charged is Mohimanul Bhuiya, who joined ISIS in 2014 but later that year emailed the FBI to alert them that he wanted to defect. He was arrested, but has since become a cooperative source and is one of very few people who have served with and left ISIS.

Among those who support or are suspected of sympathizing with ISIS, are men and women from a variety of backgrounds. Understanding the appeal of ISIS is one of the most significant barriers to fighting radicalization, and the diversity of their supporters makes doing so even more difficult. Although no large-scale attacks with direct support from ISIS have been carried out in the United States, around a quarter of those who had been arrested as of 2015 were taking part in planning attacks on US soil.

CHAPTER FOUR

How We Learn About ISIS

SIS is by its nature a closed society, without relationships with states and no formal back-and-forth communication with the world. Members of the press aren't allowed into their territory either, making it difficult

Civilians who have lived under ISIS are a primary source of information on how the group governs and functions.

to know what is going on beyond the edge of their controlled areas. Information comes out of ISIS territory unpredictably, through propaganda or people who flee their control. As a result, it can be difficult to fully grasp ISIS's plan or how attacks fit into their larger framework. It can also be difficult to know how involved ISIS is in planning attacks they claim responsibility for, or even if they are involved at all.

Finding Sources

Given the secretive nature of ISIS, it can be difficult to find reliable sources that know how the group is run, what its aims are, and what the situation is like inside their territory. The group is known for executing people they believe are defecting, and ISIS fighters have massacred thousands of civilians fleeing their territory.

But some individuals have been able to get away from the group, and through them we are able to gain an understanding of the circumstances on the ground. The portrait they paint for authorities and journalists is bleak, including violent punishments carried out in public and a brutally strict interpretation of sharia law. But it also makes clear why some are willing to align with the group: ISIS offers stability in war-torn countries, particularly in Syria. The sense of order and normality that ISIS can provide in a place where chaos was once prevalent explains why some civilians are willing to make do under ISIS control, or least make the best of it given that ISIS has responded with violence against those who try to flee.

While those who succeed in fleeing ISIS are able to give a broad sense of how the group governs, fighters who defect are even more valuable sources of information. They are also rare. When defectors are able to escape ISIS (traveling, in many cases, to Turkey), they can provide information that would otherwise be nearly impossible to gather, such as the power structure of the group, what the group's next moves could be, and—most critically—why people join the group. The International Center for the Study of Violent Extremism has worked with defectors to understand the inner workings of ISIS and the lure the group has for recruits. The information the organization has been able to gain is now being used as anti-propaganda with one central message: the utopia that ISIS promises recruits is far from the reality.

SHARIA LAW

Sharia law is a core tenet of ISIS's structure, but it is also a part of Islam that is little understood. Sharia law refers to the legal system outlined in the Koran and by rulings handed down by Islamic scholars of law. It provides numerous guidelines for daily religious practice, including how and when to pray, financial advice, and clothing requirements. There are multiple leading schools of sharia thought, including four Sunni doctrines and one Shia. On a personal level, sharia is interpreted differently by all Muslims. Individuals determine for themselves what behaviors they feel best fit their own worship practices. But sharia can be imposed strictly by states or formal courts, including in Saudi Arabia or Nigeria. In some countries and under ISIS, certain violations of sharia law are punished by execution. While there is much debate about the place of sharia law in modern society, under ISIS it is used to spread fear among the populations the group controls.

Other Terrorist Groups

Another way to understand ISIS is to look at other terrorist organizations, including the Lord's Resistance Army and al-Qaeda. Both of these groups have different goals and tactics from ISIS, but both also offer clues as to how ISIS has risen to power and continued to grow. In the case of the Lord's Resistance Army, a Ugandan terrorist organization active in Africa since the 1980s, ISIS shares both their willingness to carry out massacres against civilians and the apocalyptic message that drives devotion to the group's goals.

Other terrorist groups, like the Lord's Resistance Army in Uganda, can help experts understand ISIS's motives and tactics.

ISIS also has similarities and differences with al-Qaeda, the group in which it originated. Both are Salafist jihadist groups that use terrorism as a tool to achieve their political goals. But while al-Qaeda does not want to govern areas itself, ISIS does. ISIS believes it has the potential to be a fully-fledged state, and has put out calls for doctors, engineers, and other highly skilled recruits who can help them create a governable country. Both groups call on Muslims to join them as part of their obligation to Islam and both groups use violence against civilian populations. But ISIS has taken their mission further than al-Qaeda, which in part led to the two groups' split in 2013.

Documents

In some cases, rebel or military forces fighting ISIS have been able to obtain documents from the government bodies the group has established. These documents detail resources, costs, and salaries for fighters among other information, and so are valuable tools for understanding how ISIS functions and the condition of the group. In documents authenticated in August 2016, it was shown that ISIS leadership had been struggling financially and that some in the ranks were unhappy with their pay. This kind of unrest could help those fighting ISIS by providing pressure points. It also makes clear that although ISIS puts forward an image of unity, their leaders face internal issues.

CHAPTER FIVE

How Can We Stop Attacks by ISIS?

The international community has debated how to stop ISIS and roll back their influence since 2013. Bringing an end to ISIS's global reach is crucial to ensuring peace and stability, but finding ways to

The international community, including the United States, has come together to try to find ways to counter ISIS.

39

do so has proven difficult. Finding a way to stop ISIS is complicated for many reasons, including the intersecting circumstances that allowed for their rise, their widespread ideology, and their strategic capability. There is concern that fighting ISIS could make them lash out more than they already have, making them more of a threat as they lose power. But experts do believe there are ways that attacks by ISIS can be stopped or deterred.

Stopping Radicalization

The core group of ISIS leadership and fighters in the Middle East is small, so stemming the flow of fighters joining the group is a crucial part of cutting off their strength and capability. For years the group has relied on social media to get its message to recruits around the world, and so far anti-terrorism experts and governments have struggled to respond effectively. Experts believe that there are ways to stop the radicalization process online, and that it actually starts with understanding the process by which social media is used to identify new recruits.

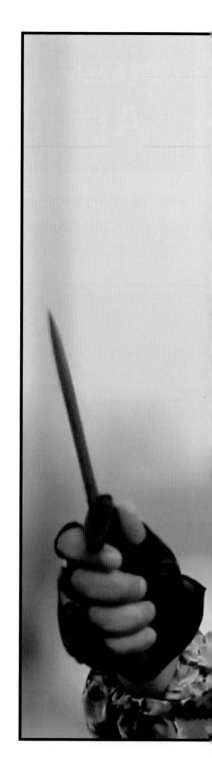

Foreign fighters who join ISIS are of particular concern, as they can easily return to their home countries to carry out attacks.

ISIS follows a predictable pattern when identifying and connecting with new recruits. According to the Brookings Institute, once a potential supporter is found, ISIS militants contact them in large numbers in order to create a small community that can amplify the group's messages. That group then encourages the potential recruit to isolate themselves by cutting ties with family or friends. At that point, the recruit is usually contacted privately, and private messages are used to determine if the recruit would be willing to travel to Syria to join fighters or carry out an attack on their own soil.

Although the final steps are done via private communication, most of the process is carried out in online groups that can be accessed. This makes it possible for analysts to observe the system by which ISIS recruits, and possibly to intervene. The earlier the intervention the better the result, and in some cases social media sites themselves can help by suspending or closing accounts that are in the early stages of contacting recruits. Other measures could be taken as well to counter ISIS propaganda and messaging.

Google is on the forefront of finding ways to identify and dissuade ISIS recruits in the earliest stages of their contact with the group. Jigsaw, a think tank and incubator owned by Google, is working on a program called the Redirect Method, which uses algorithms to determine if someone could be interested in joining ISIS. It then places anti-ISIS videos rather than advertisements in front of the user, including testimonials from defectors, Islamic leaders and scholars speaking out against ISIS, and evidence of the group's weak governance in their own territory. The Redirect Method may prove to be an important tool in the fight against radicalization and ISIS recruiting.

REFUGEES CAUGHT IN THE MIDDLE

In 2015, a refugee and migrant crisis swept Europe as more than one million people came to the continent over the course of the year, many of them fleeing the Syrian Civil War, the Libyan Civil War, and the brutality of ISIS. The current situation has been called the worst refugee crisis since the outbreak of World War II. The European Union and the United States have struggled to find a way to accommodate the

(continued on the next page)

ISIS has contributed to a refugee crisis, which has left millions without homes or resources.

(continued from the previous page)

hundreds of thousands of people who continue to use dangerous land and sea routes to get to safety, routes that have killed thousands. But refugees have become a lightning rod in politics, with some fearing that refugees could come to the United States or another European country to carry out attacks on behalf of ISIS. Studies and history have shown that refugees are extremely unlikely to carry out attacks, and are in fact fleeing the radicalism that motivates attacks. Of the over 780,000 refugees resettled in the United States since 2001, only three have been arrested on charges of terrorist activity, and none have been found to pose a credible threat to security. But fear of ISIS and their potential reach continues to cast a shadow over the refugee crisis, and makes finding solutions to the unfolding humanitarian crisis difficult.

Fighting ISIS on the Ground

Military campaigns against ideologically driven groups can be difficult, particularly when such campaigns can be used as evidence of Western aggression toward Muslims. Such propaganda can help a group like ISIS recruit more fighters by reducing the conflict to an "us versus them" mentality. Ideology is also nearly impossible to physically counter; it has to be fought with comprehensive policy that addresses not only how people who are radicalized behave, but why they were drawn to the ideology in the first place.

But ISIS does not function like other terrorist organizations, and retaking territory has real consequences for the group. When ISIS was at its height, the group was making around $30 million per month by selling oil from territory it had captured. But campaigns against the group have successfully retaken enough land or destroyed enough of their infrastructure that it is believed the group is making only $11 million per month on oil sales today. This income drop impacts the group's ability to pay fighters, provide resources, and otherwise govern properly. Without a financially reliable central government, they will struggle to support the state they hope to create and struggle to control their own forces.

Although military campaigns alone will not fully stop ISIS, weakening it by cutting off income sources and retaking territory can make the image of strength the group wants to put forward much more difficult to maintain. In turn, doing so will make their propaganda less powerful or persuasive, and recruiting new fighters will be harder.

Comprehensive Counterterrorism

Although their brutality is often difficult to understand, people join terrorist organizations like ISIS for many reasons. It is important to understand those reasons in order to create smart policy that makes ideologies of violence and destruction less appealing. In the Middle East, this means ensuring that young men and women have access to opportunity, that states are democratic and representative, and that the ongoing conflicts that have made the region unstable come to an end.

ISIS rose out of a turbulent time in the Middle East. The Arab Spring protests of 2011 had given hope to many young people in Egypt, Syria, Tunisia, Libya, and elsewhere who hoped to usher in a new era of

Ending the Syrian Civil War is crucial to fighting ISIS, but no solution

democracy in their home countries. But in most cases, states have remained authoritarian or collapsed into civil conflict. The chaos of Syria provided an incubator for ISIS to grow in, and disillusionment with their ability to effect change drove some young people to join the group.

In order to stop ISIS, it is critical that the Syrian Civil War be brought to an end—a crisis that has plagued the international community since 2011 and shows no signs of being resolved. But until the Syrian conflict is resolved, ISIS will have a safe haven from which to plan and attack. Similarly, countries like Iraq must ensure that their governments represent all citizens, and that policy works to help the young, educated populations that are today struggling to make progress toward their goals. Stability and prosperity will make radical cults like ISIS less appealing, and provide a foundation on which generations to come can build a strong, safe Middle East.

CHAPTER SIX

The Future of ISIS

S ince 2013, ISIS has gone from a small branch of a larger terrorist organization to the leading international threat of our time. This meteoric rise makes it difficult to know what could come next and, with so many issues surrounding ISIS, finding a way to combat the group effectively has caused ongoing debate among world leaders.

Balancing privacy and the need to track possible ISIS recruits is both crucial and very difficult to implement.

ISIS is able to survive for a few reasons. One reason is the continued flow of fighters willing to join their ranks or carry out attacks in their names. This allows them to spread their influence even as they lose territory in the Middle East. Another is their affiliate network, which gives the group a foothold in countries across Asia and Africa. Affiliates, though largely independent, are cells that can carry on the ISIS message if core leadership is killed in air strikes or provide safe haven if the group is forced out of their current strongholds. The third reason, and perhaps the hardest to counter, is the instability in Syria and northern Iraq. Without stability, groups like ISIS will continue to thrive due to the lack of efficient security and safety for civilians.

PEOPLE'S PROTECTION UNITS

Since the earliest days of the fight against ISIS, Kurdish fighters have been at the very front lines. Kurds are an ethnic minority in countries across the Middle East, including Iraq, Syria, and Iran. Groups called People's Protection Units, or YPG when using the Kurdish acronym, have worked with US, Syrian rebel, Turkish, and other forces to engage ISIS in direct conflict to retake roads, villages, and other areas that slowly chip away at the group's ability to gather income or spread their influence.

(continued on the next page)

(continued from the previous page)

Kurdish fighters, including these female YPG fighters, have been on the forefront of the fight against ISIS.

These groups make up the backbone of a local militia coalition called the Syrian Democratic Front (SDF) that the United States and its allies are hoping can combat ISIS directly as they slowly retake territory. Although retaking territory is one small step of what must be a larger program to defeat ISIS, through both the YPG and the SDF Syrians, Iraqis, and others are able to use their expertise to help take back their countries.

There are no easy answers to any of these questions, and given the volatile situation in Syria it is difficult to say with any certainty what could happen in the months and years to come. But many experts agree that a political solution, as opposed to a military solution, in Syria is the only logical place to start. If a political solution can be reached and stability restored to the war-torn country, then a stronger coalition can emerge and efforts can be focused on defeating ISIS. A political solution will also reduce ISIS's ability to draw recruits and reduce the likelihood that another, similar group will replace ISIS in the near future.

If a solution can be found to the conflict in Syria, other policies can be put in place to counter radicalism and defeat the remaining fighters on the ground. But since the attacks of September 11, it has become clear that terrorism has to be combated with comprehensive policies that address not just the attacks themselves, but the reasons people join groups like ISIS in the first place. If the world can find a way to stem the flow of recruits for ISIS, al-Qaeda, and any future groups with similar missions, then we can finally begin to stop terrorism for good.

Timeline

▶ **2001** On September 11, 2001, terrorists hijack four planes in the United States and use them to carry out attacks against the World Trade Center and the Pentagon, killing 2,996; the War in Afghanistan begins in October and will last until 2014.

▶ **2003** American forces invade Iraq and begin the Iraq War, which will last until 2011.

▶ **2004** Abu Musab al-Zarqawi pledges his extremist group to al-Qaeda, forming al-Qaeda in Iraq (AQI).

▶ **2006** Al-Zarqawi is killed in air strikes; Abu Mayyab al-Masri and Abu Omar al-Baghdadi become leaders of the Islamic State in Iraq (ISI).

▶ **2010** Masri and Baghdadi are killed in air strikes; Abu Bakr al-Baghdadi becomes the leader of ISI.

▶ **2011** Arab Spring protests sweep across the Middle East, upsetting long-established power structures and beginning civil conflicts, including the Syrian Civil War.

▶ **2012** In January, ISI and al-Qaeda create al-Nusra Front in Syria.

▶ **2013** Baghdadi breaks away from al-Qaeda due to long-standing disagreements and attempts to take control of al-Nusra Front; he renames ISI the Islamic State in Iraq and Syria (ISIS) and successfully takes over the city of Fallujah in Iraq.

▶ **2014** ISIS takes control of Mosul, Iraq's second-largest city; on May 24, an attack at the Brussels Jewish Museum of Belgium is carried out on behalf of ISIS.

▶ **2015** ISIS claims responsibility for downing Metrojet Flight 9268 between Egypt and Russia on October 31, which kills 217 people; on November 13, attacks on multiple sites in Paris carried out by ISIS supporters kill 139 people.

▶ **2016** An attack in Brussels, Belgium, carried out by ISIS supporters linked to the previous year's Paris attacks kills thirty-two people; Iraqi forces with US military support begin a campaign to drive ISIS out of its last stronghold in Mosul.

▶ **2017** Iraqi forces continue to fight against ISIS in Mosul; in January, the Iraqi government declares that eastern Mosul has been liberated.

affiliates Independent groups that align with larger organizations and support their mission.

al-Nusra Front A branch of al-Qaeda in Syria that was established in 2010 by Baghdadi and al-Qaeda leaders.

al-Qaeda An Islamist organization founded in the 1990s by Saudi Osama bin Laden.

al-Shabaab An Islamist terrorist organization established in Somalia in 2006 that is currently aligned with al-Qaeda.

Boko Haram An Islamist terrorist organization established in Nigeria in 2009 that is currently aligned with ISIS.

caliphate Another term for the Islamic Empire, or a state that encompasses the entire Muslim community. It has been used by ISIS to promote themselves as the leader of all Muslims, despite being rejected by the vast majority of Muslims.

ideology Beliefs and views that inform someone's behaviour and opinions.

Islamic Empire The empire that was established after the death of the Prophet Muhammad in 632 CE.

Islamic State of Iraq and Syria (ISIS) An extremist organization that was established in 2006; also known as the Islamic State (IS), the Islamic State of Iraq and the Levant (ISIL), and Daesh.

jihadist A militant and extremist strain of Islam followed by a minority of Muslims.

Kurdish An ethnic minority found in Iran, Iraq, Syria, and other regional states.

Lord's Resistance Army A Christian cult and terrorist organization formed in Uganda in 1987, led by Joseph Kony.

millenarian An ideology built on the belief that the end of the world is coming soon.

propaganda Forms of media and information that promote a particular point of view or support a mission.

radicalization The process by which someone comes to accept extremist beliefs.

Salafist An ultra-conservative branch of Sunni Islam dated to the eighteenth century that has inspired extremist groups in the modern era.

Sanaa Province An affiliate of ISIS that, like other affiliates, has taken on a name that derives from their location; Sanaa Province is named for the capital of Yemen, the country where the group is located.

sharia law Guidelines for behaviour and punishments for crimes set out in Islamic teachings.

terrorist Someone who uses violence and fear to achieve political goals.

Yazidi A Kurdish religious minority that has long been persecuted, most recently by ISIS.

Canadian Coalition Against Terror (C-CAT)
32320 Yonge Street, Suite 1219
Toronto, ON M4N 3P6
Canada
(416) 788-4777
Website: www.c-catcanada.org
C-CAT is an organization formed of ordinary Canadians, victims or family
    members of victims of terrorist attacks, as well as counterterrorism
    professionals. C-CAT aims to build bridges between the public and
    private sectors in Canada in order to better combat terrorism.

Council on Foreign Relations (CFR)
58 East 68th Street
New York, NY 10065
(212) 434-9400
Website: http://www.cfr.org
This US-based think tank brings together more than seventy research
    fellows who analyse major foreign policy issues, including terrorist
    threats, in order to better inform US policy abroad.

The Global Center on Cooperative Security (GCCS)
747 Third Avenue, 4th floor
New York, NY 10017
Website: www.globalcenter.org
GCCS is a nonprofit and nonpartisan policy institute that aims to coordinate
    counterterrorism effects at home and abroad.

Mackenzie Institute
PO Box 338, Adelaide Station
Toronto, ON M5C 2J4
Canada
(416) 686-4063
Website: http://www.mackenzieinstitute.com
This Toronto-based conservative think tank specializes in the study of
extremism and terrorism in order to inform Canadian policy. It aims to
increase Canadian military funding in order to combat terrorist
threats abroad.

National Counterterrorism Center (NCTC)
1500 Tysons McLean Drive
McLean, VA 22102
Website: https://www.nctc.gov
The NCTC was created by executive order in 2004 and aims to combat
terrorism in the United States and abroad through analyzing terrorist
threats and bringing together research and communication from
different governmental departments.

US Department of State (DOS)
2201 C Street, NW
Washington, DC 20520
(202) 647-4000
Website: http://www.state.gov
The US Department of State is an executive department that advises the
president and government on foreign policy, including military conflicts
and terrorist threats abroad. The State Department is also responsible
for maintaining international relationships.

Washington Institute on Near East Policy
1111 19th Street, NW, Suite 500
Washington, DC 20036
(202) 452-0650
Website: http://www.washingtoninstitute.org
This think tank focuses on US policy in the Middle East and regional
    issues, including combating extremism and ISIS.

Websites

Because of the changing nature of internet links, Rosen Publishing has
developed an online list of websites related to the subject of this book. This
site is updated regularly. Please use this link to access this list:

http://www.rosenlinks.com/TER21/isis

For Further Reading

Bodden, Valerie. *The Arab Spring*. New York, NY: Creative Education, 2016.

Byman, Daniel. *Al-Qaeda, the Islamic State, and the Global Jihadist Movement*. New York, NY: Oxford University Press, 2015.

Croce, Nicholas. *Anarchism, Revolution, and Terrorism*. New York, NY: Rosen Publishing, 2015.

Docalavich, Heather. *Antiterrorism Policy and Fighting Fear*. Broomall, PA: Mason Crest Publishing, 2015.

Etheredge, Laura. *Iraq*. New York, NY: Rosen Publishing, 2011.

Etheredge, Laura. *Syria, Lebanon, and Jordan*. New York, NY: Rosen Publishing, 2011.

Kennan, Caroline. *The Rise of Isis: The Modern Age of Terrorism*. New York, NY: Lucent Press, 2017.

Marsico, Katie. *ISIS*. New York, NY: ABDO Publishing Company, 2015.

Netzley, Patricia D. *Terrorism and War in the 2000s*. San Diego, CA: ReferencePoint Press, 2014.

Radu, Michael. *Islamism and Terrorist Groups in Asia*. Broomall, PA: Mason Crest Publishing, 2014.

Woolf, Alex. *Terrorism*. New York, NY: Rosen Publishing, 2011.

Bibliography

Atwan, Abdel Bari. *Islamic State: The Digital Caliphate*. Oakland, CA: University of California Press, 2015.

Berger, J. M. and Jessica Stern. *ISIS: The State of Terror*. New York, NY: HarperCollins, 2016.

Cockburn, Patrick. *The Rise of ISIS*. New York, NY: Verso, 2015.

Engel, Richard and Malcolm Nance. *Defeating ISIS: Who They Are, How They Fight, What They Believe*. New York, NY: Skyhorse Publishing, 2016.

Gerges, Fawaz A. *ISIS: A History*. Princeton, NJ: Princeton University Press, 2016.

Griffin, Michael. *Islamic State: Rewriting History*. London, UK: Pluto Press, 2016.

Hassan, Hassan and Michael Weiss. *ISIS: Inside the Army of Terror*. New York, NY: Regan Arts, 2015.

Lister, Charles R. *The Syrian Jihad*. New York, NY: Oxford University Press, 2015.

Maher, Shiraz. *Salafi Jihadism: The History of an Idea*. New York, NY: Oxford University Press, 2016.

McCants, William. *The ISIS Apocalypse*. New York, NY: St. Martin's Press, 2015.

McCoy, Terrence. "How ISIS Leader Abu Bakr al-Baghdadi Became the World's Most Powerful Jihadist Leader." *Washington Post*, June 11, 2014. https://www.washingtonpost.com/news/morning-mix/wp/2014/06/11/how-isis-leader-abu-bakr-al-baghdadi-became-the-worlds-most-powerful-jihadi-leader/?utm_term=.c630658a782e.

Micallef, Joseph V. *Islamic State: Its History, Ideology, and Challenge*. Vancouver, Canada: Antioch Downs Press, 2015.

Warrick, Joby. *Black Flags: The Rise of ISIS*. New York, NY: Penguin Random House, 2015.

Wood, Graeme. "What ISIS Really Wants." *The Atlantic*, March 2015. http://www.theatlantic.com/magazine/archive/2015/03 /what-isis-really-wants/384980.

Wright, Lawrence. *The Terror Years: From al-Qaeda to the Islamic State*. New York, NY: Knopf, 2016.

Index

About the Author

Bridey Heing is a writer and book critic based in Washington, DC. She holds degrees in political science and international affairs from DePaul University and Washington University in Saint Louis. Her areas of focus are comparative politics and Iranian politics. Her master's thesis explores the evolution of populist politics and democracy in Iran since 1900. She has written about Iranian affairs, women's rights, art, and politics for publications like *The Economist, Hyperallergic*, and *The Establishment*. She also writes about literature and film. She enjoys traveling, reading, and exploring the many museums of Washington, DC.

Photo Credits

Cover, p. 1 Moadh al-Dulaimi/AFP/Getty Images; back cover and interior pages background aleksandr hunta/Shutterstock.com (smoke), Alex Gontar/Shutterstock.com (grunge); pp. 4–5 Defne Karadeniz/Getty Images; p. 8 Universal History Archive/Universal Images Group/Getty Images; pp. 11, 17, 43 Anadolu Agency/Getty Images; pp. 12–13 Sebastian Meyer/Corbis News/Getty Images; p. 20 Fethi Belaid/AFP/Getty Images; pp. 23, 40–41 AFP/Getty Images; p. 25 Adam Berry/Getty Images; pp. 28–29 Katherine Welles/Shutterstock.com; pp. 32–33 Marcus Yam/Los Angeles Times/ Getty Images; pp. 34, 50 Ahmad al-Rubaye/AFP/Getty Images; p. 37 Adam Pletts/Getty Images; p. 39 Getty Images; pp. 46–47 The Asahi Shimbun/ Getty Images; p. 48 Kenzo Tribouillard/AFP/Getty Images.

Designer: Nicole Russo-Duca; Editor & Photo Researcher: Elizabeth Schmermund